Karl Marx

A Life from Beginning to the End

The Biography

History Hub

CONTENTS

Part One: Editor Foreword

"Those who don't know history are doomed to repeat it." — Edmund Burke
More than ever, it is important that we equip ourselves with the power of knowledge to learn from the lessons of mistakes from the past to ensure that we do not fall victim to similar mistakes. It is our aim to provide quality history books for readers to learn important history lessons critical for everyone. And we'd like to make sure you learn the stories faster, and more efficiently.

This is why we are constantly updating our catalog with new releases in History Hub. You can access the catalog of all the new titles here.

Thanks for reading,
History Hub

Chapter One: Birth and Early Childhood

Did You Know?

During Karl Marx's younger years, he frequently drank and got into fights. At the beginning of 1835, Marx attended the University of Bonn and was introduced to the didactics of Georg Wilhelm Friedrich Hegel, a philosopher, professor, and a prominent icon of German idealism. After Hegel's death in 1831, German intellectuals established an organization called The Young Hegelians, which caught Marx's interest. This group held radical views on a variety of issues, particularly religion, politics, and society. Marx was still in a rough situation at the time, causing him to get imprisoned for being involved in a brawl with a fellow student and for insobriety. His involvement with the organization radicalized him and changed his life's trajectory. Because of his extreme religious and political views and his association with The Young Hegelians, the government denied him an academic career. Consequently, he was forced to settle on a career in journalism instead.

†††

On the 5th of May 1818, Karl Heinrich Marx was born in 664 Brückergasse in Trier, a town in the Kingdom of Prussia's Lower Rhine, a province in present-day Germany. Both his parents, Herschel Marx and Henrietta Pressburg were descendants of rabbinical families. After receiving a secular education, Herschel practiced law and provided a comfortable life for his family. In 1819 as Herschel Marx commenced his career as a lawyer, he moved his family near the Porta Nigra in a ten-room property. Before his son's birth, and to escape the constraints of anti-Semitic legislation, Herschel converted from Judaism to Lutheranism, the common branch of Protestant religion in Germany and Prussia. He then took the German name Heinrich and dropped his original Yiddish birth name. His wife Henrietta Pressburg, a catachrestic Dutch Jewish, was known for her excessive motherly love, devoting much time to her family, and to the strict governance of their family home. She came from a prosperous family of entrepreneurs that later founded the company Philips Electronics. In 1824, when Karl was six years old, his father had him baptized into the same religion along with his surviving siblings, Henriette, Sophie, Hermann, Louise, Emilie, and Karoline.

Largely irreligious, Karl's father became a disciple of the The Age of Enlightenment, a loosely organized group of prominent French thinkers called "philosophes" in the mid-18th century. He was a fervent supporter of the ideas of philosophers like Leibniz, Voltaire, Kant and Lessing and introduced their ideologies and the Greek and German classics to the young Marx. Their relationship as father and son remained close almost until Heinrich's death.

There are only few historical records about Karl Marx's childhood. Despite him being born as the third out of nine children, Marx had to act like the oldest son when Moritz died in 1819. The young Karl was initially taught by his father until in 1830 when he entered Trier Gymnasium, whose headmaster, Hugo Wyttenbach, was an acquaintance of his father. The secondary school's program was of the traditional curriculum consisting of history, mathematics, literature, and languages, mainly Latin and Greek. He became exceptionally adept in Latin and French, both of which he learned how to read and write eloquently. He also taught himself other languages and thus was able to read and understand English, Italian, Spanish, Dutch, Russian, and Scandinavian. He especially mastered the English language even though he never lost his heavy German accent. He adored Shakespeare, whose works he knew by heart. He was able to finish secondary school at the age of 17. Despite growing in an overly religious extended family, he later became an atheist and a materialist, rejecting Christian and Jewish teachings. Marx even expressed his view on Religion later in life. He was saying that religious suffering is, at very much the same as the expression of genuine misery and dissent against anguish. Religion for him is the murmur of the oppressed creature or animal, the core of a cutthroat world, and the soul of soulless conditions.

When the Marx family were still in Trier, their next-door neighbor and future father-in-law Johann Ludwig von Westphalen heavily influenced Marx's early philosophy. Von Westphalen was a distinguished upper-class Prussian government official and a great admirer of the Enlightenment and its liberal ideas. Westphalen befriended his father, Heinrich Marx, wherein the children of both families, particularly Edgar and his future spouse Jenny von Westphalen and Sophie and Karl Marx, became close friends as well. Johann Ludwig von Westphalen was a polyglot and was exceedingly well-versed in both ancient and modern philosophy and literature, knowing Homer by heart, which is something Karl is keen on, with that being said, Von Westphalen became his mentor. Von Westphalen encouraged him, loaned him books, and took him on long walks to discuss lofty ideals about various philosophies and books. He talked to him about Shakespeare and Miguel de Cervantes, a Spanish writer widely regarded as the most excellent writer in the Spanish language and the author of Don Quixote. He also taught Marx social doctrines such as Saint-Simoniansm, an ideology suggesting that the state should own all property and that laborers are entitled to this based on the quality and amount of their work.

Fireside Question 1

†††

Marx grew up in an overly religious extended family and was baptized as a Lutheran at the age of six. Why did he choose to be an atheist later in his life? What ideologies influenced his non-subscription to religious teachings?

†††

The young Karl was initially taught by his father until in 1830 when he entered Trier Gymnasium, whose headmaster, Hugo Wyttenbach, was an acquaintance of his father. The secondary school's program was of the traditional curriculum consisting of history, mathematics, literature, and languages, mainly Latin and Greek. How did his education at the Trier Gymnasium encouraged his inclination towards learning foreign languages?

Fireside Question 3

†††

Marx's father was a fervent supporter of the ideas of philosophers like Leibniz, Voltaire, Kant and Lessing. He introduced their ideologies and the Greek and German classics to the young Marx. Their relationship as father and son remained close almost until Heinrich's death. Which among his father's influences do you think was vital to shaping Marx's beliefs and perspectives in life? How?

Fireside Question 4

†††

Marx's early philosophy was heavily influenced by his next-door neighbor and future father-in-law, Johann Ludwig von Westphalen, a distinguished upper-class Prussian government official and a great admirer of the Enlightenment and its liberal ideas. What was von Westphalen's role in the cultivation and enrichment of Marx's young mind?

Fireside Question 5

✝✝✝

Von Westphalen also taught Marx social doctrines such as Saint-Simoniansm, an ideology suggesting that the state should own all property and that laborers are entitled to this based on the quality and amount of their work. How did Saint-Simoniansm become the foundation for Marxism? What is its central ideology?

Chapter Two: Adolescence, Teenage & Adult Years

Did You Know?

Having a "weak chest," Marx avoided military service. Marx dodged military conscription because of his "weak chest", a condition undoubtedly exacerbated by his late-night partying, unhealthy diet, alcoholism, and chain-smoking. His father actually suggested, through a letter, that Marx consult with competent and well-known physicians to secure health certificates that would help exempt him from military service.

†††

With hopes of studying literature and philosophy, Marx flew to the North Rhine-Westphalia to study at the University of Bonn in 1835. However, his father insisted that he should take law as it was a practical field. Shortly after his 18th birthday, the military exempted him from military service due to his "weak chest." While at the university, he grew more interested in literature and philosophy rather than law and developed a strong desire to become a poet and dramatist. He even wrote a great deal of poetry in his student days—most of them preserved—that he evaluated as imitative and unremarkable later in life.

He spent a year at Bonn frequently partying and drinking instead of actually studying.

Marx's university life was eventful and fraught with trouble. He joined the Poets' Club, an organization consisting of intellectuals and social radicals who opposed long-established institutions and ideas, including religion, philosophy, and ethics. Aside from this, he also joined Landsmannschaft der Treveraner, Trier Tavern Club's drinking society, where he served as co-president at one point. He was also involved in several disputes. In August 1836, he got into an argument with the university's Borussia Korps member. Although his first term grades were good, they soon deteriorated. He also accumulated massive debts due to his excessive drinking.

Marx's "wild rampaging in Bonn" led his father to transfer him to the more scholastically oriented University of Berlin, where academic rigor was prioritized over extracurricular activities. The philosopher Ludwig Feuerbach had observed while studying there ten years earlier that one won't be able to find any other university with such a passion for work as the University of Berlin. It is no wonder that Marx's father was so eager to sign the necessary papers consenting his son's move to the capital.

From the summer to the autumn of 1836, Marx became more serious about his life and studies. However, this short period of peace was abruptly disrupted when he fell in love with his childhood friend, Jenny von Westphalen, the daughter of Baron Ludwig von Westphalen. The love story between a well-educated 22-year-old baroness and a Jewish bourgeois who is four years younger may seem very unlikely. Still, Marx befriended Jenny's father and later dedicated his doctoral thesis to Mr. Von Westphalen. Although his relationship with Jenny was socially unacceptable at that time due to their class and religious differences, their engagement still pushed through.

In October 1836, Marx arrived in Berlin, enrolling in the university's law faculty while renting a room in the Mittelstrasse. While he was studying law, philosophy also fascinated him and looked to combine the two, believing that it is impossible to accomplish anything without philosophy. His political inclination and increasing radicalism caused great anxiety to his father who expressed his concerns, in a series of letters, over his son's "demons." Heinrich admonished Marx for not taking the responsibilities of marriage seriously enough, especially when his fiance came from the upper class.

During Marx's time at the University of Berlin, he was introduced to the philosophy of G.W.F. Hegel, a former professor at the said institution. He was not initially enamored by Hegel's ideas but gradually adopted the ideology after being acquainted with the Young Hegelians, a radical group of students who criticized the prevailing political and religious establishments at that time. Its members included Bruno Bauer, a German philosopher and theologian and Ludwig Feuerbach, also a German philosopher and anthropologist, best known for his book The Essence of Christianity, which effectively criticized Hegel for his materialist philosophy. Feuerbach believed that matter or presence was inferior and subordinate to the mind or spirit, advancing the concept of "Absolute Spirit" as a projection of "the real man standing on the foundation of nature." After four years in Berlin, Marx received his doctorate from the University of Jena in 1841.

On the 15th of October 1842, Marx became an editor of a newspaper founded in Cologne, the Rheinische Zeitung ("Rhenish Newspaper"), wherein he wrote editorials on various social and economic issues, ranging from the Berlin poor's housing and the theft by peasants to the rising popularity of communism. He found the Hegelian idealism of little use in these matters. At the same time, he was growing distant from his friends at the Young Hegelians, whose social activities seemed too frivolous for the bourgeoisie. Consequently, Marx grew more attached to the "liberal-minded practical men who were struggling for freedom within the limits of the constitution." They succeeded in trebling his newspaper's circulation and making it a leading gazette in Prussia. However, the Prussian authorities halted it for being too abrupt and outspoken.

From that point forward, Marx had taken absolute moral standards and universal principles for granted. He condemned censorship as a moral evil that preyed on the weak and spied on the peoples' minds and hearts with its presupposed omniscience.

Fireside Question 6

†††

Shortly after his 18th birthday, Marx was exempted from military service due to his "weak chest." While at the University of Bonn, he grew more interested in literature and philosophy and developed a strong desire to become a poet and dramatist. What do you think could have happened if Marx pursued literature instead? Who influenced his love for poetry? .

†††

Marx's university life was eventful and fraught with trouble. Although his first term grades were good, they soon deteriorated. He also accumulated massive debts due to his excessive drinking. What do you think was the reason behind Marx's troublesome behavior at Bonn? How does this connect to his relationship with his father?

Fireside Question 8

†††

Marx's "wild rampaging in Bonn" led his father to transfer him to the more scholastically oriented University of Berlin, where academic rigor was prioritized over extracurricular activities. Should educational institutions solely focus on academics? What are the benefits of extracurricular activities to students?

†††

From the summer to the autumn of 1836, Marx became more serious about his life and studies. However, this short period of peace was abruptly disrupted when he fell in love with his childhood friend, Jenny von Westphalen, the daughter of Baron Ludwig von Westphalen. Why was their relationship socially unacceptable at the time?

†††

Marx was not initially enamored by Hegel's ideas but gradually adopted the ideology after being acquainted with the Young Hegelians, a radical group of students who criticized the prevailing political and religious establishments at that time. What was the central ideology believed by the Young Hegelians? How was this reflected or refuted in the basic tenets of Marxism?

Chapter Three: Career, Professional and Family Life

Did You Know?

He had a controversial marriage with an aristocrat childhood friend. Several years before Marx was born, his father befriended Ludwig von Westphalen, a liberal Prussian aristocrat. Marx met his daughter, Jenny Von Westphalen, when they were aged one and five, respectively. When Von Westphalen was 22, she canceled her previous betrothal to another young aristocrat and became engaged to Marx instead despite the gap in their social class. At that time in Prussia, men marrying older women were unacceptable, but that didn't hinder their love. In 1843, after years of engagement, they finally got married.

†††

After a seven-year engagement, Marx finally married Jenny von Westphalen in a Protestant church in Kreuznach on the 19th of June 1843. His extreme political views prevented him from securing a teaching position at universities. Instead, he turned to writing and journalism to support himself and his family. However, his journalistic work reflected his unorthodox sentiments, which editors and publications largely avoided.

While working in Paris, Marx was appalled by the working-class Parisians' poverty, but admired their comradeship. He later declared himself a communist and argued that the proletariat would eventually become the emancipators of society. He also became close friends with Friedrich Engels, an author who shared his condemnation of capitalism. In 1844, he published the journal Franco-German Annals, which was immediately banned in Germany. He later identified the four types of alienation in a capitalistic society and believed that the only solution to the disproportionate wealth distribution was communism. He started using the theory of alienation in his Philosophic and Economic Manuscripts of 1844, which were unpublished in his lifetime. Marx depicted the worker as suffering from four types of alienation in labor under capitalism. First, the product, over which he had no control, is always determined by the capitalist. Secondly, the production process is controlled and regulated by the business' administration. Third, while working, he does not belong to himself but to the system which provides him his wage. As he cannot develop the other sides of his personality, he has to work as a cog in a gigantic production apparatus. Lastly, the laborer is alienated from other workers, for they are pitted against each other for "higher wages" and a competitive labor market rather than encouraging a collective effort for society's betterment. Marx's alienation theory is "one of the most influential concepts of his early work."

In January 1845, Marx was deported from France at the instigation of the Prussian government. He then moved to Brussels, Belgium, where he founded the German Workers' Party, the first socialist political party for laborers in the country. He and Engels were also active in the Communist League, an international political party headed by Karl Schapper formed through a coalition with the Communist Correspondence Committee. Due to his involvement with the communists, he was also banished from Belgium.

In 1848, he published the Communist Manifesto together with Engels. This laid the foundation for the modern communist movements, anticipating that capitalism would inevitably self-destruct, would give way to the transitory state of socialism, and ultimately evolve into communism. He then met Moses Hess in one of the socialist meetings he attended to educate himself about the adversities the German working-class faced. Having learned the basic principles of socialism and its solutions for the woes of the proletariat, Marx moved back to Cologne in June 1848, where he became the editor of Neue Rheinische Zeitung: Organ der Demokratie (New Rhenish Newspaper: Organ of Democracy). After a year, the Prussian government stopped the paper and again exiled him. Marx sought refuge in Paris but was again forced to leave in September 1848. He finally settled in London, England, where he lived as a stateless exile because Britain denied him citizenship, and Prussia declined to re-naturalize him.

In London, Marx, whose sole means of living was journalism, wrote for both English and German language publications. He was a correspondent for the New York Daily Tribune, contributing a total of about 355 articles from August 1852 to March 1862. However, writing paid very poorly, making it hard for him to make ends meet. He was saved from starvation by the financial support of his friend and fellow writer, Friedrich Engels. In 1864, Marx founded the International Workingmen's Association, also known as the First International, for which he wrote an inaugural address. After that, his political activities became limited mainly to exchanging letters with leftists in Europe and America, offering them advice, and shaping socialist and labor movements. Marx spent most of his time in the British Museum researching for both his newspaper articles and books and reading available work on economic principles and monetary policies. He later published Das Kapital (The Capital) and A Critique of Political Economy, which served as the foundational theoretical text for materialist philosophy, economics, and politics. In Das Kapital, the theory of exploitation was further developed. Marx claimed that the capitalist system would eventually self-destruct due to its inability to generate profit at a sustainable level without exploiting the workers. Upon the downfall of capitalism, the proletariat would gain control of the economy. This theoretical text also served as a dialectical investigation into the forms value relations take. He also discussed his theories on the cycles of economic growth and development, the two-sector models, crisis theory and other essential elements of the Marxian political economy.

In terms of his personal life, the Marxes had seven children, four of whom died in infancy or childhood. He deeply cherished his daughters—Laura, Jenny, and Eleanor—who, in turn, adored him. Eleanor was a dynamic British labor organizer while the other two were married to Frenchmen who were prominent socialists, communists, and members of Parliament.

Marx's extreme smoking, wine drinking, and love for intensely spicy food contributed to and triggered his illnesses, which rendered him unable to continue scholarly work in his later years. He died in his armchair in London on the 14th of March 1883, about two months before his 65th birthday. He lies buried in London's Highgate Cemetery, where a bust mark his grave.

Fireside Question 11

†††

Marx's extreme political views prevented him from securing a teaching position at universities. Instead, he turned to writing to support himself and his family. However, his journalistic work reflected his unorthodox sentiments, which editors and publications largely avoided. What did Marx write about in his articles? Why were they considered radical?

††

While working in Paris, Marx was appalled by the working-class Parisians'
poverty, but admired their comradeship. He later declared himself a communist
and argued that the proletariat would eventually become the emancipators of
society. What led Marx to become a communist? What was his central
ideology? Do you think his principles are correct given that communism has
barely survived into modern society?

Fireside Question 13

†††

Marx identified the three types of alienation in a capitalistic society and believed that the only solution to the disproportionate wealth distribution was communism. What are the three types of alienation in capitalism? Why does Marx view capitalism as evil? How could communism solve the problems of a capitalistic society according to him?

Fireside Question 14

†††

Marx's keen interest was guided and encouraged by Westphalen, who loaned Marx books, and took him on long walks in which he talked to him about Miguel de Cervantes, Don Quixote, and Shakespeare. How did this interest manifest in his career choices later on in life?

†††

Marx spent most of his time in the British Museum researching for both his newspaper articles and books and reading available work on economic principles and monetary policies. He later published Das Kapital (The Capital) and A Critique of Political Economy, which served as the foundational theoretical text for materialist philosophy, economics, and politics. What are the economic theories that Marx put forth in Das Kapital? How did communist countries put these theories into practice? Discuss why these countries failed and why they reverted back to socialism or capitalism.

Chapter Four: Main Difficulties to Overcome in Life

Did You Know?

Marx was a man without a nation. Throughout the 1840s, orders that Marx should leave a country within 24 hours was all around Europe as he kept on getting banned from one country to another. It started in 1843 when Tsar Nicholas I, the Emperor of Russia, ordered the government to stop the publication of Rheinische Zeitung, a radical left newspaper edited by Marx. He was forced to leave Prussia and headed to France, but in 1845, the French government closed his periodical, Vorwarts, and deported him. In 1849, he again fled to France, but the government sent him packing, and so he sought refuge in England with his wife who was pregnant with their fourth child. However, Britain denied him citizenship, and Prussia declined to re-naturalize him. Nonetheless, he built a life in England but died a stateless person.

†††

In the 18th-century, Karl Heinrich Marx was born in a middle-class family. The history of his childhood and youth, the phase of life before his Abitur exam in 1835, is essentially "lost." He never kept a diary or composed memoirs of his youth, and there are no eyewitness reports of his childhood. Not even isolated observations or letters by relatives, acquaintances, or teachers have survived. Even later, when Marx was recognized for his ideologies, none of his acquaintances published any recollections of him. Only his youngest daughter, Eleanor, shared two anecdotes after his death, both unspecific in terms of period. Otherwise, only a few pieces of information can be gleaned from official documents. Despite this biographical gap, he is considered as one of the most influential figures in human history. Hailed as a "man of science," he also made two significant discoveries: "the development law of human history" and "the special law of motion governing the present-day the capitalist mode of production." Above all, he is considered the founding father of modern socialism.

Before achieving all the accolades and recognition, Marx had to make numerous sacrifices, and encountered seemingly insurmountable challenges. His first obstacle was choosing a career path. Originally wanting to be a poet and dramatist, he ended up taking law upon the recommendation of his father. More problems came up when instead of studying, he spent his time drinking and getting into fights. His misfortune continued even after pursuing a career in journalism when publications turned down his articles due to his extreme political views. His involvement in several communist organizations also made him a target of criticism and of government ire. Believing that communism would provide an indispensable instrument for the necessary emancipation of the working class, he continued his scholarly work at the expense of his family.

Continuously exiled from one country to another, pursued by angry creditors and without permanent lodging, Marx and his family lived in dire and abject poverty. They barely managed to survive on a small income from his writing stints and Engels' support. He also dealt with the loss of three out of his seven children: Heinrich, 14 days old, Edgar, eight years old and Franziska, one year old, due to severe malnutrition. He even had no money to pay for a coffin until a fellow refugee came to his rescue. He and his family were afflicted by various illnesses, some of which stemmed from their miserable condition. Jenny, his oldest daughter, also died a year later due to cancer.

Marx's thirst for knowledge was never quenched and he still voraciously read books despite his old age. In 1878-1883, he studied mathematics, agrochemistry, geology, ground rent and agrarian relations, organic and inorganic chemistry, and taught himself new languages such as Russian and Turkish. He later developed a catarrh that kept him ill for fifteen months and eventually progressed into bronchitis and pleurisy. He died in an armchair in his study in London on the 14th of March 1883. A stateless person, Marx was buried in Highgate Cemetery, London, on the 17th of March 1883. His epitaph reads: "workers of all lands unite."

Fireside Question 16

†††

The history of Marx's childhood and youth, the phase of life before his Abitur exam in 1835, is essentially "lost." He never kept a diary or composed memoirs of his youth, and there are no eyewitness reports of his childhood. Despite this biographical gap, how do you think has Marx's family background and childhood predisposed him into empathizing with the working class?

Fireside Question 17

†††

Hailed as a "man of science," he made two significant discoveries: "the development law of human history" and "the special law of motion governing the present-day the capitalist mode of production." Above all, he is considered the founding father of modern socialism. Briefly discuss the two laws. How do they connect to the basic tenets of socialism?

Fireside Question 18

†††

Marx's first obstacle was choosing a career path. Originally wanting to be a poet and dramatist, he ended up taking law upon the recommendation of his father. Have you encountered the same dilemma? What does this say about society in general? Does this kind of problem persist until today?

Fireside Question 19

†††

Marx's misfortune continued even after pursuing a career in journalism when publications turned down his articles due to his extreme political views. His involvement in several communist organizations also made him a target of criticism and of government ire. What was the state of press freedom back in the 19th century? Do you think that modern society progressed or stagnated in terms of freedom of speech?

Fireside Question 20

††

A stateless person, Marx was buried in Highgate Cemetery, London, on the 17th of March 1883. His epitaph reads: "workers of all lands unite." With the downfall of communism, do you think that it rendered Marx's contributions meaningless? What principles from communism could still work in a capitalistic society?

Chapter Five: Inspiration and Influence behind Person and Work

Did You Know?

Marx relied on Engels for money. Marx lived in Paris for two years—the hotbed for political thought in the mid-19th century—where he met Friedrich Engels, a wealthy German philosopher, historian, communist, political scientist, journalist, political activist, and businessman, at the Café de la Régence and started one of the most critical philosophical friendships in modern times. Engels shaped Marx's perspective on the proletariat with his real-world experience as the owner of his family's textile mill. They collaborated on several essays, including The Communist Manifesto, an 1848 political document that encapsulated Marx and Engels' theories regarding the nature of society and politics, predicting how the capitalist society would eventually shift to socialism. Engels provided the money to publish Das Kapital in 1867. This foundational theoretical text proposed that the life-blood of capitalism lies in the unjust profiteering of capitalists from their laborers, who receive compensation, which is less than the actual value they add to the products they made.

Aside from that, Engels also regularly gave the struggling Marx money for his family. Ironically, the well-off industrialist reaped the benefits of his workers' labor while aiding Marx in championing a system that would depose his capitalist advantage.

In 1883, Marx died penniless with just eleven people at his funeral. He suffered from headaches, eye inflammation, joint pain, insomnia, liver and gallbladder problems, and depressive symptoms. He referred to his numerous health problems as "the wretchedness of existence." Marx's pain was exacerbated by his bad habits, such as eating foods which are bad for the liver, working late nights, and excessive smoking and drinking. Despite his situation, Marx kept up the pace of his work. But the condition that ultimately killed him at the age of 64 was his "weak chest" which may have been induced by pleurisy, an inflammation of the lungs and throat.

†††

The revolutionary philosopher and radical thinker, Karl Heinrich Marx, did not live long enough to see his ideas carried out. Still, his works and writings established the theoretical basis for modern international communism. Marx received inspiration through various channels and people in his life, which inspired him to conceptualize some of the world's most groundbreaking ideas that remain highly influential until today. These people include:

Heinrich Marx (1777 – 1838)

Heinrich Marx, the father of Karl Heinrich Marx, was a passionate Prussian patriot, and a well-respected lawyer in Trier, whose income allowed his family to live comfortably as liberal Lutherans. Heinrich, a reasonable and rational man by nature, had his son educated at home until the age of twelve. He introduced the young Marx to the great philosophies of the Greek and German classics.

Johann Ludwig von Westphalen (the 11th of July 1770 – the 3rd of March 1842)

Von Westphalen was considered as the mentor and role model of Marx, who referred to him as a "dear fatherly friend." He imbued Marx with enthusiasm for literature, especially for the works of Homer and Shakespeare, who became Marx's favorite author. He spent much of his time with the young Marx reading Voltaire and Racine and going for intellectual walks through "the hills and woods." He also introduced Marx to the socialist teachings of Saint-Simon.

Marx dedicated his doctoral thesis, The Difference Between the Democritean and Epicurean Philosophy of Nature, written in 1841, to von Westphalen in an effusive manner. He even wrote a letter to his friend relating how he stood as a father figure who had always been the living proof that idealism is no illusion. In 1842, Marx was present during von Westphalen's last moments.

Georg Wilhelm Friedrich Hegel (1770-1831)

Hegel was the most notable philosopher in Germany during his time and his views were widely taught to and highly regarded by his students. Marx studied under Hegel's pupil, Bruno Bauer, a young philosopher who was the Young Hegelians' leader. There are different ways to evaluate the influence Hegel cast over Marx. Some consider it as a significant catalyst in the formation of Marx's investigations, while others saw it as an enticement to unscientific speculation.

Marx's philosophy on historical materialism was undoubtedly greatly influenced by Hegel's dialectics on history as an ongoing struggle for freedom. He argued that history is dictated not by human ideals and consciousness but by the prevailing means of production and economics drivers of the time. He encapsulated the "materialist conception of history" in the 1859 preface of A Contribution to the Critique of Political Economy, outlining a societal framework consisting of a "base" and a "superstructure". Marx elucidated how capitalism emerged from feudalism and how a capitalistic society would eventually correct itself by necessity and ultimately shift into communism.

Immanuel Kant (1724–1804)

Kant is believed to have the most significant influence on modern-day philosophers. Kantian philosophy was the foundation of Marxism. Hegel's dialectical method, which Marx appropriated, was an extension of reasoning from Kant's antinomies.

Ludwig Andreas von Feuerbach (1804 – 1872)

In 1841, his book The Essence of Christianity was published, explaining Feuerbach's ideology and critique of religion, which later gained recognition. Feuerbach is also known as a philosopher and anthropologist. This work was the foundation of Marx's early philosophy on religion. However, Marx's first encounter with the critique of religion did not begin with Feuerbach, but rather with the controversies around Hegel's philosophy of faith in the 1830s. To understand these debates, the upheavals experienced by the Christian faith and Protestant theology in the late 18th century must be considered.

Adam Smith (1723 – 1790) and David Ricardo (1772 – 1823)

Adam Smith, an economist, philosopher, author, and moral philosopher, was an icon of the Scottish Enlightenment. A pioneer of political economy, he is known as "The Father of Economics" or "The Father of Capitalism." Marx critique Smith and Ricardo for not realizing that their economic concepts reflected specifically capitalist institutions, not inherent natural properties of human society, and could not be applied universally to all communities.

This theoretical distinction was Marx's primary insight and allowed him to develop the concept of" surplus value," which was eminent in his works compared to Smith and Ricardo. Marx explained that the value of a worker's labour is incommensurately compensated by the capitalist and this remuneration is only enough to sustain the worker on a day-to-day basis. He asserted that capitalists take advantage of the proletariat by unjustly appropriating the "surplus value" or uncompensated value that workers add to their products.

In Das Kapital, the theory of exploitation was further developed. Marx claimed that the capitalist system would eventually self-destruct due to its inability to generate profit at a sustainable level without exploiting the workers. Upon the downfall of capitalism, the proletariat would gain control of the economy. This theoretical text also served as a dialectical investigation into the forms value relations take. He also discussed his theories on the cycles of economic growth and development, the two-sector models, crisis theory and other essential elements of the Marxian political economy.

Fireside Question 21

†††

Marx received inspiration through various channels and people in his life, which influenced him to conceptualize some of the world's most groundbreaking ideas that remain highly influential until today. Among all the people listed above, who do you think had the most impact on Marx and played the most vital role? Why is that so?

Fireside Question 22

†††

Marx's philosophy on historical materialism was undoubtedly greatly influenced by Hegel's dialectics on history as an ongoing struggle for freedom. What is the basic assertion of Marx's historical materialism? How did it differ from the idealists' conception of history?.

Fireside Question 23

†††

Marx elucidated how capitalism emerged from feudalism and how a capitalistic society would eventually correct itself by necessity and ultimately shift into communism. How did feudalism morph into capitalism? What are the inherent weaknesses of a capitalistic society?

†††

Marx explained that the value of a worker's labour is incommensurately compensated by the capitalist and this remuneration is only enough to sustain the worker on a day-to-day basis. He asserted that capitalists take advantage of the proletariat by unjustly appropriating the "surplus value" or uncompensated value that workers add to their products. Do you still observe this exploitative nature of capitalism until today? Cite some modern-day examples.

†††

Adam Smith has a significant influence on Marxian economics, specifically in the accumulation of the surplus-value theory and then developing the idea of exploitation through Das Kapital. Do you think that the principle stated in Das Kapital is still applicable up to this day? Why or why not?

Chapter Six: Main Accomplishments and Notable Achievements

Did You Know?

His novels and love poems were unpublished during his lifetime. Beyond his political philosophy and scholarly works in economics, Marx also wrote several love poems to Von Westphalen, a play set in Italy's mountain town, and a satirical novel called Scorpion and Felix. None of his fiction saw the light of day during his lifetime, and Scorpion and Felix only survived in fragments, but all of these were published posthumously in the 50-volume set of Marx and Engels's Collected Works.

†††

Karl Heinrich Marx was a German philosopher, journalist, economist, and revolutionary. He is considered one of the world's most influential figures due to the impact of his theories on economic, intellectual, and political progress. His most acclaimed works include the Communist Manifesto, also known as the Communist Party's Manifesto and Das Kapital, which served as the foundational theoretical text for communist philosophy, economics, and politics. His most significant theories include historical materialism and the exploitation and alienation of the proletariat under capitalistic conditions. Marx is proclaimed as one of the fathers of modern socialism and sociology, for his works in economics laid the foundation for today's understanding of labor and its relation to capital.

Karl Marx developed the theory of alienation of workers under capitalism. The notion of "separation" is integral to Marx's early writings. He started using the theory of alienation in his Philosophic and Economic Manuscripts of 1844, which were unpublished during his lifetime. Marx depicts the worker under capitalism as suffering from alienation in labor—from other human beings, the products of their labor, and the act of labor itself.

Karl Marx's theory of historical materialism is considered one of his most significant contributions. It is elucidated most comprehensively in Die Deutsche Ideologie (The German Ideology), a set of manuscripts and compositions written by Marx and Engels in 1846. His theory of history sees human society as being fundamentally determined at any given time by its material conditions or the connection and relationships which people have with each other for producing and reproducing the means of human existence. His theory of history revolved around the possibility that forms of society rise and fall and then impede human productive development. He identified six successive stages of building up these material conditions in Western Europe: through primitive communism, slave society, feudalism, socialism, capitalism, and communism. He thoroughly examined capitalism as if he lived in this stage.

Marx's concept of class struggle was highly influential. Rather than conceiving society as being based on consensus, Marx established a conflict model of social systems, stating that "class struggle is the tension in society due to competing socioeconomic interests and desires between people of different classes." Marx believed that class struggle played a "crucial role in the history of class-based hierarchical systems." He identified capitalist society as containing two main social groups: the laborers, who earn their livelihood by selling their labor power and have little choice but to work, and the capitalists, who get their income from the surplus value they appropriate from the workers who create wealth. Class struggle is key to Marx's theory of history and had an enormous influence on sociology and culture study.

Marx co-authored The Communist Manifesto with Freidrich Engels. In 1846, the Communist Corresponding Committee was established in Brussels by Marx and his close friend Friedrich Engels. On the other hand, in Paris circa 1836, The League of the Just, a socialist group founded by German émigrés, formed a coalition with the Communist Corresponding Committee to create the Communist League in June 1847, an international political party that remained until 1852. On the 21st of February 1848, Marx and Engels jointly wrote the Communist Manifesto, which had preambles divided into four sections. Marx's materialist conception of history is stated in the first section while the second section expressed the party's will to defend the world's working class' common interests. The third section differentiated communism from other socialist doctrines prevalent at the time. And lastly, the fourth section discussed the communist position on class struggles occurring in various countries during the mid-nineteenth century.

The Communist Manifesto is regarded as one of the most influential political texts. Its massive influence was initially restricted within Germany during the Europe-wide revolutions in 1848. It was then published across the continent and some parts of the world in 30 languages throughout the 1870s and 1910s. The "focal belt of Europe" from Russia in the east to France felt its greatest ideological impact. Following the Russian Revolution's success, the world's first socialist state was founded explicitly along Marxist lines and required the political class to study the Communist Manifesto. The text gained acclaim across the world and entered political-science syllabuses of many universities. The manifesto remained widely read even after the collapse of the Soviet Bloc in the 1990s. Many consider it a valuable insight into the society in which we live today and explain today's world of repeated economic crises and recurrent wars.

Marx wrote the groundbreaking three-volume theoretical text Das Kapital. In 1867, he released the first volume, the second one in 1885 and the third volume was published by Friedrich Engels after Marx's death. The work's principal idea is that capitalism's life-blood is in the exploitation of laborers, whose unpaid work is the ultimate surplus value source. According to Marx, the massive unemployment and the consequent labor surplus drove wage rates to the minimum level that could only support the laborer's daily necessities—a state preferred by capitalists as it promoted the accumulation of capital. The capitalist system is destined to self-destruct due to its inherent unsustainability and when the capitalists lose hold of the power, the proletariat will inherit the control over society and the working class would take over key economic and political decisions.

Marx was a leading member of the First International. In 1864, the organization International Workingmen's Association (IWA) was founded in

London. IWA, also known as First International, had a substantial influence as a consolidation force for labor in Europe during the late 19th century. Marx himself was a key member and authored the organization's documents. Based on records reported, the organization has around 8 million members at its peak. IWA played a vital role when the French government held Paris down on the 18th of March 1871 for 76 days due to a rebellion. During this time, the city was governed by a radical socialist and revolutionary government known as the Paris Commune. The French army ultimately suppressed the Commune. The Civil War in France, which is one of his most famous pamphlets, written in response to this bloody uprising, was about the character and significance of the struggle of the Communards during the Paris Commune. In 1872, the IWA started to fall apart and split into two. The socialist wing was led by Marx and the anarchist faction led by Mikhail Bakunin.

Marx's works in economics laid the foundation for understanding labor and its relation to capital. He stated that "economic science cannot exist independently from history and sociology," and that "there is no eternal economic law as it changes with production". Thus, to reduce financial problems into something purely material was considered mystification, and a sense of historical relativism characterized his financial analysis. His well-known theories include the Labor Theory of Value (LTV), which argues that " the economic value of a good or service is determined through the total amount of necessary labor required to produce it". Political economics based on Marx's philosophies is known as Marxian economics. Some of its concepts like capital accumulation and the business cycle are used in capitalism. His scholarly work influenced subsequent economic thought and laid the foundation for the understanding of the relationship between labor and capital.

Marx is one of the founding fathers of modern sociology. Social science is a major academic discipline concerning society and the relationships among individuals within a community. The main social sciences include political science, economics, demography, and sociology. Sociology is construed as the systematic study of human and cultural actions. Along with Émile Durkheim, Auguste Comte and Max Weber, Karl Marx is considered one of the four fathers of modern sociology.

In contrast to other sociologists, Marx constructed theories that could often be tested using the scientific method. Critical concepts of Marxist sociology include historical materialism, modes of production, and the relation between capital and labor. It is primarily concerned with, though not limited to, the way economics defined social roles and expectations. Marx's notion of metabolic rift, which occurs due to ecological crisis instigated by the unsustainability of capitalism, is considered as the predecessor of modern ecological thought.

Marx was one of the most prominent figures throughout history. His works influenced economic, intellectual, and political thought during the 19th century. The following century saw revolutions in many countries that labeled themselves Marxists, most notably the Russian Revolution, which led to the world's first socialist state, the Soviet Union. Prominent world leaders, including Vladimir Lenin, Fidel Castro, and Mao Zedong, cited Marx as an influence. However, there were modifications to his original ideas, and many movements have not been faithful to his works. Marx also provided a critique of 19th-century capitalism. Many believe that his theories on exploitative relationships between capitalists and their employees remain valid until today.

Even though Marx remains a controversial figure, he still is regarded as one of history's greatest thinkers.

Fireside Question 26

†††

Marx's most significant theories include historical materialism and the exploitation and alienation of the proletariat based on class struggle. Marx is proclaimed as the father of modern socialism, for his works in economics laid the foundation for today's understanding of labor and its relation to capital. What do you think is Marx's most significant accomplishment? Why is that so?

†††

What is the essence of his most influential theoretical works such as The Communist Manifesto and Das Kapital? How did these books shape our understanding of labor, value and their effects on society's structure?

Fireside Question 28

†††

Rather than conceiving society as being based on consensus, Marx established a conflict model of social systems, stating that "class struggle is the tension in society due to competing socioeconomic interests and desires between people of different classes." How is the concept of class struggle still relevant today?

Fireside Question 29

†††

Prominent world leaders, including Vladimir Lenin, Fidel Castro, and Mao Zedong, cited Marx as an influence. However, there were modifications to his original ideas, and many movements have not been faithful to his works. How did these leaders implement Marx's concepts? Where did they fail?

Fireside Question 30

†††

Marx's notion of metabolic rift, which occurs due to ecological crisis instigated by the unsustainability of capitalism, is considered as the predecessor of modern ecological thought. Why is the capitalist system ecologically unsustainable? Could technological advancement be a remedy to this? Cite examples.

Dear reader,

It was my utmost privilege performing a deep dive to bringing this book for you today.

Before saying goodbye, I'd like to take opportunity to offer you one final gift. If you've enjoyed this book, may I ask for a small favor of a review?

Even a few sentences would help a lot and tell others more about this book.

If you do, as a way of showing my utmost appreciation,I'll send you for FREE a most cherished and valuable gift:

Top 7 Bestsellers Treasure Box

These are my personal bestsellers sold at bookstores valued at ~$30USD, my gift to you absolutely FREE.

To claim your gift:

1. Leave a review where the book was purchased
2. Send a screenshot to irvinepress@mail.com
3. Receive your gift of **Top 7 Bestsellers Treasure Box**

We've prepared the best and hope you'll find this offer exciting! Hope to see you again soon.

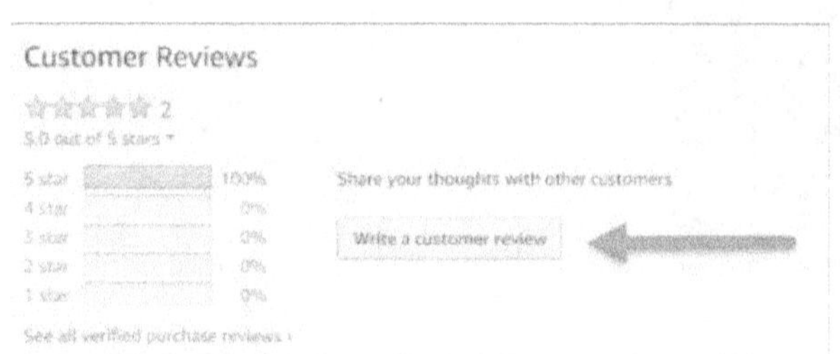

THANK YOU